French

Made Nice & Easy!

Staff of Research & Education Association
Carl Fuchs, Language Program Director

Based on Language Courses developed by the
U.S. Government for Foreign Service Personnel

Research & Education Association
Dr. M. Fogiel, Director
61 Ethel Road West
Piscataway, New Jersey 08854

FRENCH MADE NICE & EASY

Printed in the United States of America

Library of Congress Control Number 00-109909

International Standard Book Number 0-87891-364-5

What This Guide Will Do For You

Whether travelling to a foreign country or to your favorite international restaurant, this *nice & easy* guide gives you just enough of the language to get around and be understood. Much of the material in this book was developed for government personnel who are often assigned to a foreign country on a moment's notice and need a quick introduction to the language.

In this handy and compact guide, you will find useful words and phrases, popular expressions, common greetings, and the words for numbers, money, and time. Every word or phrase is accompanied with the correct pronunciation and spelling. There is a vocabulary list for finding words quickly. Generous margins on the pages allow you to make notes and remarks that you may find helpful.

To provide perspective into the language and country, the book begins with the country's history. If you expect to travel there in the future, you will also appreciate the section of up-to-date facts on the country.

By keeping this guide in your pocket or purse, you'll be well prepared to converse as well as understand this new language.

Carl Fuchs
Language Program Director

Contents

FRANCE

Facts & History

Official Name: French Republic

Geography: Area: 551,670 sq. km. (220,668 sq. mi.); largest west European country, about four-fifths the size of Texas. Cities: *Capital*—Paris. *Other cities*—Marseille, Lyon, Toulouse, Strasbourg, Nice, Bordeaux. Terrain: Varied. Climate: Temperate; similar to that of the eastern U.S.

People:
Nationality: *Adjective*—French.
Population: 58 million.
Annual growth rate: 0.5%.
Ethnic groups: Celtic and Latin with Teutonic, Slavic, North African, Indochinese, and Basque minorities.
Religion: Roman Catholic 90%.
Language: French.
Education: *Years compulsory*—10. *Literacy*—99%.
Health: Infant mortality rate—7/1,000.
Work force (25 million): *Services*—66%. *Industry and commerce*—28%. *Agriculture*—6%.

Government:

Type: Republic.

Constitution: September 28, 1958.

Branches: *Executive*—president (chief of state); prime minister (head of government).

Legislative—bicameral Parliament (577-member National Assembly, 319-member Senate). *Judicial*—Court of Cassation (civil and criminal law), Council of State (administrative court), Constitutional Council (constitutional law).

Political parties: Rally for the Republic (Gaullists/conservatives); Union for French Democracy (a center-right conglomerate of 5 parties: Democratic Force, Republican Party, and Radical Party are the three major components.) Socialist Party; Communist Party; National Front; Greens; Ecology Generation; various minor parties.

History of France

Since prehistoric times, France has been a crossroads of trade, travel, and invasion. Three basic European ethnic stocks—Celtic, Latin, and Teutonic (Frankish)—have blended over the centuries to make up its present population.

The French language derives from the vernacular Latin spoken by the Romans in Gaul, although it includes many Celtic and Germanic words. French has been an international language for centuries and is a common second language throughout the world. It is one of five official languages at the United Nations. In Africa, Asia, the Pacific, and the West Indies, French has been a unifying factor, particularly in those countries where it serves as the only common language among a variety of indigenous languages and dialects.

France was one of the earliest countries to progress from feudalism into the era of the nation-state. Its monarchs surrounded themselves with capable ministers, and French armies were among the most innovative, disciplined, and professional of their day. During the reign of Louis XIV (1643-1715), France was the dominant power in Europe. But overly ambitious projects and military campaigns of Louis and his successors led to chronic financial problems in the 18th century. Deteriorating economic conditions and popular resentment against the complicated system of privileges granted the nobility and clerics were among the principal causes of the French Revolution (1789-94).

Although the revolutionaries advocated republican and egalitarian principles of government, France reverted to forms of absolute rule or constitutional monarchy four times—the Empire of Napoleon, the Restoration of Louis XVIII, the reign of Louis-Philippe, and the Second Empire of Napoleon III. After the Franco-Prussian War (1870), the Third Republic was established and lasted until the military defeat of 1940. World War I (1914-18) brought great losses of troops and materiel. In the 1920s, France established an elaborate system of border defenses (the Maginot Line) and alliances to offset resurgent German strength.

France was defeated early in World War II, however, and occupied in June 1940. The German victory left the French groping for a new policy and new leadership suited to the circumstances. On July 10, 1940, the Vichy government was established. Its senior leaders acquiesced in the plunder of French resources, as well as the sending of French forced labor to Germany; in doing so, they claimed they hoped to preserve at least some small amount of French sovereignty. The German occupation proved quite costly, however, as a full one-half of France's public sector revenue was appropriated by Germany. After 4 years of occupation and strife, Allied forces liberated France in 1944. A bitter legacy carries over to the present day.

France emerged from World War II to face a series of new problems. After a short period of provisional government initially led by Gen. Charles de Gaulle, the Fourth Republic was set up by a new constitution and established as a parliamentary form of government controlled by a series of coalitions. The mixed nature of the coalitions and a consequent lack of agreement on measures for dealing with Indochina and Algeria caused successive cabinet crises and changes of government. Finally, on May 13, 1958, the government structure collapsed as a result of the tremendous opposing pressures generated in the divisive Algerian issue. A threatened coup led the Parliament to call on General de Gaulle to head the government and prevent civil war. He became prime minister in June 1958 (at the beginning of the Fifth Republic) and was elected president in December of that year.

Seven years later, in an occasion marking the first time in the 20th century that the people of France went to the polls to elect a president by direct ballot, de Gaulle won re-election with a 55% share of the vote, defeating Francois Mitterrand. In April 1969, President de Gaulle's government conducted a national referendum on the creation of 21 regions with limited political powers. The government's proposals were defeated, and de Gaulle subsequently resigned. Succeeding him as president of France have been Gaullist Georges Pompidou (1969-74), Independent Republican Valery Giscard d'Estaing (1974-81), Socialist Francois Mitterrand (1981-95), and neo-Gaullist Jacques Chirac (elected in spring 1995).

While France continues to revere its rich history and independence, French leaders are increasingly tying the future of France to the continued development of the European Union. During President Mitterrand's tenure, he stressed the importance of European integration and advocated the ratification of the Maastricht Treaty on European economic and political union, which France's electorate narrowly approved in September 1992.

President Jacques Chirac assumed office May 17, 1995, after a campaign focused on the need to combat France's stubbornly high unemployment rate. The center of domestic attention soon shifted, however, to the economic reform and belt-tightening measures required for France to meet the criteria for Economic and Monetary Union (EMU) laid out by the Maastricht Treaty. In late 1995, France experienced its worst labor unrest in at least a decade, as employees protested government cutbacks. On the foreign and security policy front, Chirac took a more assertive approach to protecting French peacekeepers in the former Yugoslavia and helped promote the peace accords negotiated in Dayton and signed in Paris in December 1995. The French have been one of the strongest supporters of NATO and EU policy in Kosovo and the Balkans.

France's birth rate was among the highest in Europe from 1945 until the late 1960s. Since then, its birth rate has fallen but remains higher than that of most other west European countries. Traditionally, France has had a high level of immigration. About 90% of the people are Roman Catholic, less than 2% are Protestant, and about 1% are Jewish. More than 1 million Muslims emigrated in the 1960s and early 1970s from North Africa, especially Algeria. At the end of 1994, there were about 4 million persons of Muslim descent living in France.

Pleyben Calvary

Arles, the Roman Arena

Hints on Pronunciation

You will find all the words and phrases written both in French spelling and in a simplified spelling which you read like English. Don't use the French spelling, the one given in parentheses, unless you have studied French before. *Read the simplified spelling as though it were English.* When you see the French word for "where" spelled *oo*, give the *oo* the sound it has in the English words *too*, *boot*, etc. and not the sound it has in German or any other language you may happen to know.

Each letter or combination of letters is used for the sound it usually stands for in English and it *always* stands for that sound. Thus, *oo* is always pronounced as it is in *too*, *boo*, *boot*, *tooth*, *roost*, never as anything else. Say these words and then pronounce the vowel sound by itself. That is the sound you must use every time you see *oo* in the *Pronunciation* column. If you should use some other sound—for example, the sound of *oo* in *blood*—you might be misunderstood.

Syllables that are accented, that is, pronounced louder than others, are written in capital letters. In French, unaccented syllables are not skipped over quickly, as they are in English. The accent is generally on the last syllable in the phrase.

Hyphens are used to divide words into syllables in order to make them easier to pronounce. Curved lines (‿) are used to show sounds that are pronounced together without any break; for example, *day-z‿UH* meaning "some eggs," *kawm-B‿YANG* meaning "how much?"

Special Points

AY	as in *may, say, play* but don't drawl it out as we do in English. Since it is not drawled it sounds almost like the *e* in *let*. Example: *ray-pay-TAY* meaning "repeat."
J	stands for a sound for which we have no single letter in English. It is the sound we have in *measure, leisure, usual, division, casualty, azure*. Example: *bawn-JOOR* meaning "Good day."

EW	is used for a sound like *ee* in *bee* made with the lips rounded as though about to say the *oo* in *boot*. Example: *ek-skew-zay MWA* meaning "Excuse me."
U or UH	as in *up, cut, rub, gun*. Examples: *nuf* meaning "nine," *juh* meaning "I."
<u>*U*</u> or <u>*UH*</u>	as in *up, cut*, etc. but made with the lips rounded. Example: *D<u>UH</u>* meaning "two."

The difference between these two sounds is not too important in French and you will be understood if you use the vowel in *up* in all cases. The *uh* which is pronounced like the vowel in *up* but with the lips rounded is underlined in the *Useful Words and Phrases* so that you can compare the two sounds as you listen to the record.

NG, N or M	are used to show that certain vowels are pronounced through the nose, very much in the way we generally say *huh, uh-uh, uh-huh*. Examples: *lahnt-MAHNG* meaning "slowly," *juh kawm-PRAHNG* meaning "I understand," *NAWNG* meaning "no," *PANG* meaning "bread."

Memory Key

AY	as in *day* but not so drawled.
U *or* UH	as in *up*.

5

EW	for the sound in *bee* said with the lips rounded.
J	for the sound in *measure, division*.
NG, N *or* **M**	for vowels pronounced through the nose.

Calais, Town Hall

Chateau d'Angers

GREETINGS AND GENERAL PHRASES

English	*Pronunciation and French Spelling*
Hello *or* **Good day**	*bawn-JOOR* (Bonjour)

Notice the sound of *j* in the word *JOOR*. Listen again and repeat: *JOOR, JOOR*. It is the same sound we have in *measure, usual, division, azure,* etc. We have no single letter for this sound in English, so we write it in your *Language Guide* as *j*. But remember—always pronounce *j* as you heard it in *JOOR*, never as the *j* in *judge*. Try just the sound again: *j, j*.

English	Pronunciation and French Spelling
Good evening	*bawn-SWAR* (Bonsoir)
How are you?	*kaw-MAHN-T͜ah-lay VOO?* (Comment allez-vous?)
Sir	*muss-YUH* (Monsieur)
Madam	*ma-DAHM* (Madame)
Miss	*mad-mwa-ZEL* (Mademoiselle)
Please	*SEEL voo PLAY* (S'il vous plaît)
Excuse me	*ek-skew-zay MWA* (Excusez-moi)
You're welcome	*eel nee ah pa duh KWA* (Il n'y a pas de quoi)
Yes	*WEE* (oui)
No	*NAWNG* (non)

In the last word you heard a sound pronounced through the nose. Listen again and repeat: *NAWNG, NAWNG*. In English we often have a somewhat similar sound when we say *huh, uh-uh, uh-huh*. The vowel sounds that must be pronounced through the nose like this are written in your *Guide* with an *ng* or *n*, and in a few cases, *m* after them. Always remember, however, that these letters are there only to remind you to pronounce the vowels through the nose. Try just the sound again: *AWNG, AWNG*.

Do you understand?	*KAWM-pruh-nay VOO?* (Comprenez-vous?)
I understand	*JUH kawm-PRAHNG* (Je comprends)

English	Pronunciation and French Spelling
I don't understand	*juh nuh KAWM-prahng PA* (Je ne comprends pas)
Speak slowly, please	*par-lay LAHNT-mahng, seel voo PLAY* (Parlez lentement; s'il vous plaît)
Please repeat	*RAY-pay-tay, seel voo PLAY* (Répétez s'il vous plaît)

LOCATION

When you need directions to get somewhere you use the phrase "where is" and then add the words you need.

Where is	*oo AY* (Où est)
the restaurant	*luh RESS-to-RAHNG* (le restaurant)
Where is the restaurant?	*oo AY luh RESS-to-RAHNG?* (Où est le restaurant?)
the hotel	*lo-TEL* (l'hôtel)
Where is the hotel?	*oo AY lo-TEL?* (Où est l'hôtel?)
the railroad station	*la GAR* (la gare)
Where is the railroad station?	*oo AY la GAR?* (Où est la gare?)

9

English	Pronunciation and French Spelling
the toilet	*luh la-va-BO* (le lavabo)
Where is the toilet?	*oo A Y luh la-va-BO?* (Où est le lavabo?)

DIRECTIONS

The answer to your question "Where is such and such?" may be "To the right" or "To the left" or "Straight ahead," so you need to know these phrases:

To the right	*ah DRWAT* (à droite)
To the left	*ah GOHSH* (à gauche)
Straight ahead	*too DRWA* (tout droit)

It is sometimes useful to say "Please show me.

Please show me	*seel voo PLAY, mawn-tray-MWA* (S'il vous plaît, montrez-moi)

If you are driving and ask the distance to another town it will be given you in kilometers, not miles.

Kilometer	*kee-lo-METR* (kilomètre)

One kilometer equals ⅝ of a mile.

NUMBERS

You need to know the numbers.

One	*UNG*	un
Two	*DUH*	deux

English	Pronunciation and French Spelling

You have just heard a sound you should practice. It is like the *u*-sound in *up* or *but*, said with the lips rounded. Listen again and repeat: *DUH*, *DUH*. Try just the sound again: *UH*, *UH*.

English	Pronunciation	French Spelling
Three	*TRWA*	trois
Four	*KATR*	quatre
Five	*SANK*	cinq
Six	*SEESS*	six
Seven	*SET*	sept
Eight	*WEET*	huit
Nine	*NUF*	neuf
Ten	*DEESS*	dix
Eleven	*AWNZ*	onze
Twelve	*DOOZ*	douze
Thirteen	*TREZ*	treize
Fourteen	*KA-TAWRZ*	quatorze
Fifteen	*KANZ*	quinze
Sixteen	*SEZ*	seize
Seventeen	*DEESS-SET*	dix-sept
Eighteen	*DEEZ-WEET*	dix-huit
Nineteen	*DEEZ-NUF*	dix-neuf
Twenty	*VANG*	vingt

Three other vowels that are pronounced through the nose have now been used several times. You heard them in *kaw-MAHNG, VANG, UNG*. Listen again and repeat: *kaw-MAHNG, VANG, UNG*. Try just the sounds again: *AHNG, ANG, UNG*.

For "twenty-one," "thirty-one" and so on, you say "twenty and one," "thirty and one," but for "twenty-two," "thirty-two" and so on, you just add the words for "two" and "three" after the words for "twenty" and "thirty," as we do in English.

Twenty-one	*van-t̯ay UNG*	vingt-et-un
Twenty-two	*vant-DUH*	vingt-deux
Thirty	*TRAHNT*	trente
Forty	*KA-RAHNT*	quarante
Fifty	*SAN-KAHNT*	cinquante
Sixty	*SWA-SAHNT*	soixante

"Seventy," "eighty," "ninety" are said "sixty ten," "four twenties" and "four twenties ten."

Seventy	*swa-sahnt-DEESS*	soixante-dix
Eighty	*kat-ruh-VANG*	quatre-vingt
Ninety	*kat-ruh-van-DEESS*	quatre-vingt-dix
One hundred	*SAHNG*	cent
One thousand	*MEEL*	mille

Bayeux, Croquevieille Mill

Bayeux, Notre Dame Cathedral

WHAT'S THIS?

When you want to know the name of something you can say "What is it?" or "What's this?" and point to the thing you mean.

What is it?   *kess kuh SAY?*   (Qu'est-ce que c'est?)

What's this?   *kess kuh suh-SEE?*   (Qu'est-ce que ceci?)

What's that?   *kess kuh say kuh SA?*   (Qu'est-ce que c'est que çà?)

ASKING FOR THINGS

When you want something use the phrase "I want" and then add the name of the thing wanted. Always use "Please" —*seel voo PLAY.*

I want   *juh voo-DRAY*   (Je voudrais)

some cigarettes   *day see-ga-RET*   (des cigarettes)

I want some cigarettes   *juh voo-DRAY day see-ga-RET*   (Je voudrais des cigarettes)

to eat   *mahn-JAY*   (manger)

I want to eat   *juh voo-DRAY mahn-JAY*   (Je voudrais manger)

13

Here are the words for some of the things you may require. Each of them has the French word for "some" before it.

bread   *dew PANG*   (du pain)

butter   *dew BUR*   (du beurre)

soup   *duh la SOOP*   (de la soupe)

meat   *duh la V⌣YAHND*   (de la viande)

lamb   *dew moo-TAWNG*   (du mouton)

veal   *dew VO*   (du veau)

pork   *dew PAWR*   (du porc)

beef   *dew BUF*   (du boeuf)

eggs   *day-z⌣UH*   (des oeufs)

vegetables   *day lay-GEWM*   (des légumes)

In the last word you heard a sound you must practice. It is written in your *Guide* as *ew*. Listen to the word again: *lay-GEWM, lay-GEWM*. To pronounce the sound *ew*, you say *ee* but at the same time round your lips as though about to say *oo*. Try just the sound again: *ew, ew*.

potatoes   *day PAWM duh TAYR*   (des pommes de terre)

string beans   *day ah-ree-ko VAYR*   (des haricots verts)

cabbage   *day SHOO*   (des choux)

carrots   *day ka-RAWT*   (des carottes)

English	Pronunciation and French Spelling
peas	*day puh-tee PWA* (des petits pois)
salad	*duh la sa-LAD* (de la salade)
sugar	*dew SEWKR* (du sucre)
salt	*dew SEL* (du sel)
pepper	*dew PWAVR* (du poivre)
milk	*dew LAY* (du lait)
drinking water	*duh LO paw-TABL* (de l'eau potable)
a cup of tea	*ewn TASS duh TAY* (une tasse de thé)
a cup of coffee	*ewn TASS duh ka-FAY* (une tasse de café)
a glass of beer	*ung VAYR duh B‿YAYR* (un verre de bière)
a bottle of wine	*ewn boo-TAY‿ee duh VANG* (une bouteille de vin)
some matches	*day-z‿ah-lew-MET* (des allumettes)

MONEY

To find out how much things cost, you say:

How much? *kawm-B‿YANG?* (Combien?)

The answer will be given in francs, sous, and centimes.

English	Pronunciation and French Spelling

Five centimes equal one sou, twenty sous or one hundred centimes equal one franc.

centime	*sahn-TEEM* (centime)
sou	*SOO* (sou)
franc	*FRAHNG* (franc)

TIME

When you want to know what time it is you say really "What hour is it?"

What time is it?   *kel UR ay-t‿EEL?*   (Quelle heure est-il?)

For "One o'clock" you say "It is one hour."

One o'clock   *eel ay-t‿EWN UR*   (Il est une heure)

For "Two o'clock" you say "It is two hours."

Two o'clock   *eel ay DUH-Z‿UR*   (Il est deux heures)

"Ten past two" is "Two hours ten."

Ten past two   *duh-z‿UR DEESS*   (deux heures dix)

"Quarter past five" is "Five hours and quarter."

Quarter past five   *sank UR ay KAR*   (cinq heures et quart)

"Half past six" is "Six hours and half."

Half past six   *see-z‿UR ay duh-MEE*   (six heures et demie)

"Quarter of eight" is "Eight hours less the quarter."

Quarter of eight	_wee-t͜ UR mwang luh KAR_	(huit heures moins le quart)

When you want to know when a movie starts or when a train leaves, you say:

At what hour	_ah KEL UR_	(à quelle heure)
begins	_kaw-MAHNSS_	(commence)
the movie	_luh see-nay-MA_	(le cinéma)
When does the movie start?	_ah KEL UR kaw-MAHNSS luh see-nay-MA?_	(A quelle heure commence le cinéma?)
the train	_luh TRA NG_	(le train)
leaves	_PAR_	(part)
When does the train leave?	_ah KEL UR par luh TRA NG?_	(A quelle heure part le train?)
Yesterday	_ee-YA YR_	(hier)
Today	_o-joord-WEE_	(aujourd'hui)
Tomorrow	_duh-MA NG_	(demain)

The days of the week are:

Sunday	_dee-MAHNSH_	(dimanche)
Monday	_LUN-DEE_	(lundi)

17

English	Pronunciation and French Spelling
Tuesday	*MAR-DEE* (mardi)
Wednesday	*MAYR-kruh-DEE* (mercredi)
Thursday	*JUH-DEE* (jeudi)
Friday	*VAHN-druh-DEE* (vendredi)
Saturday	*SAM-DEE* (samedi)

OTHER USEFUL PHRASES

The following phrases will be useful:

What is your name? *kaw-MAHNG voo-z ah-puh-lay VOO?* (Comment vous appelez-vous?)

My name is__ *juh ma-PEL__* (Je m'appelle__)

How do you say *table* in French? *kaw-MAHNG deet voo* table *ang frahn-SAY?* (Comment dites-vous *table* en français?)

I am an American *juh SWEE-Z ah-may-ree-KANG* (Je suis Américain)

I am your friend *juh SWEE vawtr ah-MEE* (Je suis votre ami)

Please help me *ay-day MWA seel voo PLAY* (Aidez-moi s'il vous plaît)

Where is the camp? *oo ay luh KAHNG?* (Où est le camp?)

Eiffel Tower

English	Pronunciation and French Spelling
Take me there	*muh-nay-z_ee MWA* (Menez-y moi)
Good-by	*o ruh-VWAR* (Au revoir)

ADDITIONS AND NOTES

Thank you	*mayr-SEE* (merci)
I want	*juh VUH* (Je veux)

The expression given on the record—*juh voo-DRAY*—is a polite way of saying "I want"; it really means "I would like." *juh VUH* is much stronger and should be used only when making a strong request or demand.

19

ADDITIONAL EXPRESSIONS

English	*Pronunciation and French Spelling*
I am hungry	*jay FANG* (J'ai faim)
I am thirsty	*jay SWAF* (J'ai soif)
Stop!	*ALT!* (Halte!)
Come here!	*vuh-NAY-Z ee-SEE!* (Venez ici!)
Right away	*toot SWEET* (Tout de suite)
Come quickly!	*vuh-nay VEET!* (Venez vite!)
Go quickly!	*ah-lay VEET!* (Allez vite!)
Help!	*o suh-KOOR!* (Au secours!)
Help me!	*ay-day MWA!* (Aidez-moi!)
Bring help!	*ah-lay shayr-SHAY dew suh-KOOR!* (Allez chercher du secours!)
You will be rewarded	*voo suh-RAY ray-kawm-pahn-SAY* (Vous serez récompensé)
Where are the American sailors?	oo SAWNG lay mah-RANG-Z ah-may-ree-KANG? (Où sont les marins américains?)
Which way is north?	*duh kel ko-TAY ay luh NAWR?* (De quel côté est le nord?)
Which is the road to___?	*kel ay luh shuh-MANG poor___?* (Quel est le chemin pour___?)

English	Pronunciation and French Spelling
Draw me a map	*fet MWA ung kraw-KEE* (Faites-moi un croquis)
Is it far?	*ess kuh say LWANG?* (Est-ce que c'est loin?)
Take me to a doctor	*kawn-dwee-zay-MWA shay-z_ung dawk-TUR* (Conduisez-moi chez un docteur)
Take cover!	*met-ay VOO-Z_ah la-BREE!* (Mettez-vous à l'abri!)
Gas!	*gahz!* (Gaz!)
Danger!	*dahn JAY!* (Danger!)
Watch out!	*pruh-nay GARD!* (Prenez garde!)
Be careful!	*fet ah-tahnss-YAWNG!* (Faites attention!)
Wait!	*ah-tahn-DAY!* (Attendez!)
Good luck	*bawn SHAHNSS* (Bonne chance)

Chateau de Lusse on the river

FILL-IN SENTENCES

In this section you will find a number of sentences, each containing a blank space which can be filled in with any one of the words in the list that follows. For example, in order to say "I want a room," look for the phrase "I want___" in the English column and find the French expression given beside it: *juh VUH___*. Then look for "a room" in the list that follows; the French is *ewn SHAHMBR*. Put the word for "a room" in the blank space and you get *juh VUH ewn SHAHMBR*.

English	*Pronunciation and French Spelling*
I want___	*juh VUH___* (Je veux___)
We want___	*noo voo-LAWNG___* (Nous voulons___)
I'd like___	*juh voo-DRAY___* (Je voudrais___)
I need___	*eel muh FO___* (Il me faut___)
Bring me___	*ah-pawr-tay MWA___* (Apportez-moi___)
Give me___	*daw-nay MWA___* (Donnez-moi___)
Where can I get___?	*oo pweej troo-VAY___?* (Où puis-je trouver___?)
I have___	*jay___* (J'ai___)
We have___	*noo-z‿ah-VAWNG___* (Nous avons___)
We don't have___	*noo na-vawng PA___* (Nous n'avons pas___)
Have you___?	*ah-vay VOO___?* (Avez-vous___?)

English	Pronunciation and French Spelling
	EXAMPLE
I want___	*juh VUH___* (Je veux___)
boiled water	*duh LO boo-YEE* (de l'eau bouillie)
I want boiled water	*juh VUH duh LO boo-YEE* (Je veux de l'eau bouillie)

English	Pronunciation and French Spelling
bacon	*LAR* (lard)
beefsteak	*bif-TEK* (bifteck)
chicken	*poo-LAY* (poulet)
chops	*kawt-LET* (côtelettes)
lamb chops	*kawt-LET duh moo-TAWNG* (côtelettes de mouton)
pork chops	*kawt-LET duh PAWR* (côtelettes de porc)
beans	*ah-ree-KO* (haricots)
rice	*REE* (riz)
spinach	*ay-pee-NAR* (épinards)
turnips	*na-VAY* (navets)
apples	*PAWM* (pommes)
chocolate	*shaw-kaw-LA* (chocolat)

English	Pronunciation and French Spelling
fruit	*frwee* (fruit)
grapes	*day ray-ZANG* (des raisins)
oranges	*o-RAHNJ* (oranges)
a cup	*ewn TASS* (une tasse)
a plate	*ewn ahss-YET* (une assiette)
a glass	*ung VAYR* (un verre)
a knife	*ung koo-TO* (un couteau)
a fork	*ewn foor-SHET* (une fourchette)
a spoon	*ewn kwee-YAYR* (une cuillère)
a room	*ewn SHAHMBR* (une chambre)
a bed	*ung LEE* (un lit)
blankets	*day koo-vayr-TEWR* (des couvertures)
sheets	*day DRA* (des draps)
a mattress	*ung mat-LA* (un matelas)
a pillow	*un⁀aw-ray-YAY* (un oreiller)
a mosquito net	*ewn moo-stee-KAYR* (une moustiquaire)

English	Pronunciation and French Spelling
cigars	*day see-GAR* (des cigares)
a pipe	*ewn PEEP* (une pipe)
tobacco	*dew ta-BA* (du tabac)
a pen	*ewn PLEWM* (une plume)
a pencil	*ung kray-YAWNG* (un crayon)
ink	*duh LAHNKR* (de l'encre)
a comb	*ung PEN-yuh* (un peigne)
hot water	*duh lo SHOHD* (de l'eau chàude)
a razor	*ung ra-ZWAR* (un rasoir)
razor blades	*day LAM duh ra-ZWAR* (des lames de rasoir)
a shaving brush	*ung blay-RO* (un blaireau)
shaving soap	*dew sa-VAWNG ah BARB* (du savon à barbe)
soap	*dew sa-VAWNG* (du savon)
a toothbrush	*ewn BRAWSS ah DAHNG* (une brosse à dents)
tooth paste	*duh la PAHT dahn-tee-FREESS* (de la pâte dentifrice)

Chateau Azay-le-Rideau

Rouen, the Gros Horloge

English	Pronunciation and French Spelling
a towel	*ewn sayrv-YET* (une serviette)
a handker-chief	*ung moo-SHWAR* (un mouchoir)
a raincoat	*un̮am-payr-may-AHBL* (un imperméable)
a shirt	*ewn shuh-MEEZ* (une chemise)
shoes	*day sool-YAY* (des souliers)
shoe laces	*day la-SAY* (des lacets)
shoe polish	*dew see-RAJ* (du cirage)
underwear	*day soo-vet-MAHNG* (des sous-vêtements)
buttons	*day boo-TAWNG* (des boutons)
needle	*ewn ah-GWEE-yuh* (une aiguille)
pins	*day-z̮ay-PANGL* (des épingles)
safety pins	*day-z̮ay-PANGL duh sewr-TAY* (des épingles de sûreté)
thread	*dew FEEL* (du fil)
aspirin	*duh lah-spee-REEN* (de l'aspirine)
a bandage	*ung pahnss-MAHNG* (un pansement)
cotton	*dew kaw-TAWNG* (du coton)

English	Pronunciation and French Spelling
a disinfectant	*ung day-zan-fek-TAHNG* (un désinfectant)
iodine	*duh L͜Yawd* (de l'iode)
a laxative	*ung lak-sa-TEEF* (un laxatif)

I want to__	*juh VUH__* (Je veux__)
I'd like to__	*juh voo-DRAY__* (Je voudrais__)

EXAMPLE

I want to__	*juh VUH__* (Je veux__)
eat	*mahn-JAY* (manger)
I want to eat	*juh VUH mahn-JAY* (Je veux manger)

buy it	*lash-TAY* (l'acheter)
drink	*BWAR* (boire)
wash up	*muh la-VAY* (me laver)
take a bath	*prahndr ung BANG* (prendre un bain)
rest	*muh ruh-po-ZAY* (me reposer)
sleep	*dawr-MEER* (dormir)
have my hair cut	*muh fayr koo-PAY lay shuh-VUH* (me faire couper les cheveux)
be shaved	*muh fayr ra-ZAY* (me faire raser)

English	Pronunciation and French Spelling
Where is there___?	*oo ee-ah-t̮ EEL___?* (Où y a-t-il___?)
Where can I find___?	*oo pweej troo-VAY___?* (Où puis-je trouver___?)

EXAMPLE

Where is there___?	*oo ee-ah-t̮ EEL___?* (Oŭ y a-t-il___?)
a barber	*ung kwa-FUR* (un coiffeur)
Where is there a barber?	*oo ee-ah-t̮ EEL ung kwa-FUR?* (Où y a-t-il un coiffeur?)

a dentist	*ung dahn-TEEST* (un dentiste)
a doctor	*ung dawk-TUR* (un docteur)
a mechanic	*ung may-ka-neess-YANG* (un mécanicien)
a policeman	*un ah-JAHNG duh paw-LEESS* (un agent de police)
a porter	*ung pawr-TUR* (un porteur)
a servant	*ung daw-mess-TEEK* (un domestique)
a shoemaker	*ung kawr-dawn-YAY* (un cordonnier)
a tailor	*ung ta-YUR* (un tailleur)
a workman	*un oov-R YAY* (un ouvrier)
a church	*ewn ay-GLEEZ* (une église)

English	Pronunciation and French Spelling
a clothing store	*ung ma-ga-ZANG duh kawn-feks-YAWNG* (un magasin de confection)
a drugstore	*ewn far-ma-SEE* (une pharmacie)
a garage	*ung ga-RAJ* (un garage)
a grocery	*ewn ay-peess-REE* (une épicerie)
a house	*ewn may-ZAWNG* (une maison)
a laundry	*ewn blahn-sheess-REE* (une blanchisserie)
a spring	*ewn SOORSS* (une source)
a well	*ung PWEE* (un puits)

Where is___?	*oo AY___?* (Où est___?)
How far is___?	*ah kel deess-TAHNSS ay___?* (A quelle distance est___?)

EXAMPLE

Where is___?	*oo AY___?* (Où est___?)
the bridge	*luh PAWNG* (le pont)
Where is the bridge?	*oo AY luh PAWNG?* (Où est le pont?)

the bus	*lo-to-BEWSS* (l'autobus)
the city	*la VEEL* (la ville)
the highway	*la grahnd ROOT* (la grande route)
the hospital	*lo-pee-TAL* (l'hôpital)

English	Pronunciation and French Spelling
the main street	*la grahng REW* (la grand' rue)
the market	*luh mar-SHAY* (le marché)
the nearest town	*luh vee-LAJ luh plew PRAWSH* (le village le plus proche)
the police station	*luh PAWST duh paw-LEESS* (le poste de police)
the post office	*luh bew-RO duh PAWST* (le bureau de poste)
the railroad	*luh shuh-MANG duh FAYR* (le chemin de fer)
the river	*la reev-YAYR* (la rivière)
the road	*la ROOT* (la route)
the ship	*luh na-VEER* (le navire)
the telegraph office	*luh bew-RO dew tay-lay-GRAF* (le bureau du télégraphe)
the telephone	*luh tay-lay-FAWN* (le téléphone)
the town	*luh vee-LAJ* (le village)

I am___	*juh SWEE___* (Je suis___)
He is___	*eel AY___* (Il est___)

English	Pronunciation and French Spelling
We are___	*noo SAWM___* (Nous sommes___)
You are___	*voo-z_ET___* (Vous êtes___)
They are___	*eel SAWNG___* (Ils sont___)

EXAMPLE

I am___	*juh SWEE___* (Je suis___)
sick	*ma-LAD* (malade)
I am sick	*juh SWEE ma-LAD* (Je suis malade)

wounded	*blay-SAY* (blessé)
lost	*payr-DEW* (perdu)
tired	*fa-tee-GAY* (fatigué)

It is___	*SAY___* (C'est___)
Is it___?	*ess kuh SAY___?* (Est-ce que c'est___?)
It is not___	*suh nay PA___* (Ce n'est pas___)

EXAMPLE

It is not___	*suh nay PA___* (Ce n'est pas___)
good	*BAWNG* (bon)
It is not good	*suh nay pa BAWNG* (Ce n'est pas bon)

31

English	Pronunciation and French Spelling
bad	*mo-VAY* (mauvais)
expensive	*SHAYR* (cher)
too expensive	*tro SHAYR* (trop cher)
here	*ee-SEE* (ici)
there	*LA* (là)
near	*PRAY* (pres)
far	*LWANG* (loin)

Nice, Hotel Negresco

IMPORTANT SIGNS

Stop *or* Halte	Stop
Ralentir	Go Slow
Détour	Detour
Attention	Caution
Sens Unique	One Way
Sens Interdit	No Thoroughfare
Passage à Niveau	Grade Crossing
Impasse	Dead End
Tenez votre Droite	Keep to the Right
Tournant Dangereux	Dangerous Curve
Chemin de Fer	Railroad
Lignes à haute tension	High Tension Lines
Défense d'entrer	Keep Out *or* No Admittance
Défense de Fumer	No Smoking
W.C.	Toilet
Hommes	Men
Dames	Women
Entrée	Entrance
Sortie	Exit

ALPHABETICAL WORD LIST

English	Pronunciation and French Spelling

A

a *or*	*ung* (un) *ewn* (une)
am	
I am	*juh SWEE* (Je suis)
Americans	*ah-may-ree-KANG* (américains)
American sailors	mah-RANG Z‿ah-may-ree-KANG (marins américains)
I am an American	*juh SWEE-Z‿ah-may-ree-KANG* (Je suis américain)
and	*ay* (et)
apples	*PAWM* (pommes)
are	
Are you___?	*et VOO___?* (Etes-vous___?)
They are___	*eel SAWNG___* (Ils sont___)
We are___	*noo SAWM___* (Nous sommes___)
aspirin	*ah-spee-REEN* (aspirine)

English	Pronunciation and French Spelling

B

bacon	*LAR* (lard)
bad	*mo-VAY* (mauvais)
bandage	*pahnss-MAHNG* (pansement)
barber	*kwa-FUR* (coiffeur)
beans	*ah-ree-KO* (haricots)
string beans	*ah-ree-ko VAYR* (haricots verts)
bed	*LEE* (lit)
beef	*BUF* (boeuf)
beer	*b͜yayr* (bière)
a glass of beer	*ung VAYR duh B͜YAYR* (un verre de bière)
blankets	*koo-vayr-TEWR* (couvertures)
boiled water	*o boo-YEE* (eau bouillie)
bread	*PANG* (pain)
bridge	*PAWNG* (pont)
bring	
Bring help!	*ah-lay shayr-SHAY dew suh-KOOR!* (Allez chercher du secours!)

English	Pronunciation and French Spelling
Bring me___	*ah-pawr-tay MWA___* (Apportez-moi___)
brush	
shaving brush	*blay-RO* (blaireau)
bus	*o-to-BEWSS* (autobus)
butter	*BUR* (beurre)
buttons	*boo-TAWNG* (boutons)
buy it	*lash-TAY* (l'acheter)

C

cabbage	*SHOO* (chou)
can	
Where can I find___?	*oo PWEEJ troo-VAY___?* (Où puis-je trouver___?)
careful	
Be careful!	*fet ah-tahnss-YAWNG!* (Faites attention!)
carrots	*ka-RAWT* (carottes)

English	Pronunciation and French Spelling
centime	*sahn-TEEM* (centime)
chicken	*poo-LAY* (poulet)
chocolate	*shaw-kaw-LA* (chocolat)
chops	*kawt-LET* (côtelettes)
lamb chops	*kawt-LET duh moo-TAWNG* (côtelettes de mouton)
pork chops	*kawt-LET duh PAWR* (côtelettes de porc)
church	*ay-GLEEZ* (église)
cigarettes	*see-ga-RET* (cigarettes)
cigars	*see-GAR* (cigares)
city	*VEEL* (ville)
clothing store	*ma-ga-ZANG duh kawn-feks-YAWNG* (magasin de confection)
coffee	*ka-FAY* (café)
a cup of coffee	*ewn TASS duh ka-FAY* (une tasse de café)
comb	*PEN-yuh* (peigne)
Come!	*vuh-NAY!* (Venez!)
Come here!	*vuh-NAY-Z ee-SEE!* (Venez ici!)
Come quickly!	*vuh-nay VEET!* (Venez vite!)

English	Pronunciation and French Spelling
cotton	*kaw-TAWNG* (coton)
cover	
Take cover!	*met-ay VOO-Z_ah la-BREE!* (Mettez-vous à l'abri!)
cup	*TAHSS* (tasse)
a cup of__	*ewn TAHSS duh__* (une tasse de__)

D

Danger!	*dahn-JAY!* (Danger!)
day	*JOOR* (jour)
Good day	*bawng JOOR* (Bonjour)
dentist	*dahn-TEEST* (dentiste)
disinfectant	*day-zanᵣfek-TAHNG* (désinfectant)
Do you under-stand?	*KAWM-pruh-nay VOO?* (Comprenez-vous?)
doctor	*dawk-TUR* (docteur)
Take me to a doctor	*kawn-dwee-zay-MWA shay-z_ung dawk-TUR* (Conduisez-moi chez un docteur)
Draw me a map	*fet-mwa ung kraw-KEE* (Faites-moi un croquis)
(to) drink	*BWAR* (boire)

English	Pronunciation and French Spelling
drinking water	*o paw-TABL* (eau potable)
drugstore	*far-ma-SEE* (pharmacie)

E

(to) eat	*mahn-JAY* (manger)
eggs	*UH* (oeufs)
eight	*WEET* (huit)
eighteen	*DEEZ-WEET* (dix-huit)
eighty	*kat-ruh-VANG* (quatre-vingt)
eleven	*AWNZ* (onze)
excuse me	*ek-skew-zay MWA* (excusez-moi)
evening	*SWAR* (soir)
Good evening	*bawn-SWAR* (Bonsoir)
expensive	*SHAYR* (cher)

F

far	*LWANG* (loin)
Is it far?	*ess kuh SAY LWANG?* (Est-ce que c'est loin?)
How far is it?	*ah kel dee-stahnss ESS?* (A quelle distance est-ce?)

English	Pronunciation and French Spelling
fifteen	*KANZ* (quinze)
fifty	*san-KAHNT* (cinquante)
(to) find	*troo-VAY* (trouver)
Where can I find___?	*oo pweej troo-VAY___?* (Où puis-je trouver___?)
fish	*pwa-SAWNG* (poisson)
five	*SANK* (cinq)
fork	*foor-SHET* (fourchette)
forty	*ka-RAHNT* (quarante)
four	*KATR* (quatre)
fourteen	*ka-TAWRZ* (quatorze)
franc	*FRAHNG* (franc)
French	*frahn-SAY* (français)
in French	*ang frahn-SAY* (en français)
Friday	*VAHN-druh-DEE* (vendredi)
friend	*ah-MEE* (ami)
I am your friend	*juh SWEE vawtr a-MEE* (Je suis votre ami)
fruit	*frwee* (fruit)

English	Pronunciation and French Spelling

G

garage	*ga-RAJ* (garage)
get	
Where can I get___?	*oo pweej troo-VAY___?* (Où puis-je trouver___?)
Give me___	*daw-nay MWA___* (Donnez-moi___)
glass	*VAYR* (verre)
a glass of___	*ung VAYR duh___* (un verre de___)
Go!	*ah-LAY!* (Allez!)
Go quickly!	*ah-lay VEET!* (Allez vite!)
good	*BAWNG* (bon)
Good day	*bawng-JOOR* (Bonjour)
Good evening	*bawn-SWAR* (Bonsoir)
Good-by	*o ruh-VWAR* (Au revoir)
grapes	*ray-ZANG* (raisins)
grocery	*ay-peess-REE* (épicerie)

H

hair	*shuh-VUH* (cheveux)
have my hair cut	*muh fayr koo-PAY lay shuh-VUH* (me faire couper les cheveux)

Venus de Milo, Louvre

Villandry

English	Pronunciation and French Spelling
half	*duh-MEE* (demi)
half past six	*see-z͜ UR ay duh-MEE* (six heures et demi)
ham	*jahm-BAWNG* (jambon)
handkerchief	*moo-SHWAR* (mouchoir)
(to) have	*av-WAR* (avoir)
Have you?	*ah-vay VOO?* (Avez-vous?)
I have	*JAY* (J'ai)
I don't have	*juh nay PA* (Je n'ai pas)
We have	*noo-z͜ ah-VAWNG* (Nous avons)
We don't have	*noo na-vawng PA* (Nous n'avons pas)
he	*eel* (il)
He is___	*eel AY___* (Il est___)
Help!	*o suh-KOOR!* (Au secours!)
Bring help!	*ah-lay shayr-SHAY dew suh-KOOR!* (Allez chercher du secours!)
Help me!	*ay-day MWA!* (Aidez-moi!)
here	*ee-SEE* (ici)
Come here!	*vuh-NAY-z͜ ee-see!* (Venez ici!)
highway	*grahn ROOT* (grande route)

English	Pronunciation and French Spelling
hospital	*o-pee-TAL* (hôpital)
Take me to a hospital	*kawn-dwee-zay-MWA ah lo-pee-TAL* (Conduisez-moi à l'hôpital)
hot water	*o shohd* (eau chaude)
hotel	*o-TEL* (hôtel)
house	*may-ZAWNG* (maison)
how	*kaw-MAHNG* (comment)
How are you?	*kaw-MAHN-T ah-lay VOO?* (Comment allez-vous?)
How do you say___?	*kaw-MAHNG deet voo___?* (Comment dites-vous___?)
How far is it?	*ah kel dee-stahnss ESS?* (A quelle distance est-ce?)
How much?	*kawm-B YANG?* (Combien?)
hundred	*SAHNG* (cent)
hungry	
I am hungry	*jay FANG* (J'ai faim)

I

I	*juh* (je)
I have___	*JAY___* (J'ai___)

43

English	Pronunciation and French Spelling
I don't have___	*juh nay PA* (Je n'ai pas___)
I am hungry	*jay FANG* (J'ai faim)
I am thirsty	*jay SWAF* (J'ai soif)
I want___ *or* **I want to___**	*juh VUH___* (Je veux___)
I would like___	*juh voo-DRAY___* (Je voudrais___)
ink	*AHNKR* (encre)
iodine	*yawd* (iode)
is	
He is___	*eel AY___* (Il est___)
It is___	*SAY___* (C'est___)
It is not___	*suh nay PA___* (Ce n'est pas___)
Is it___?	*ess kuh SAY___?* (Est-ce que c'est___?)
Is it far?	*ess-kuh SAY LWANG?* (Est-ce que c'est loin?)
What is it?	*kess kuh SAY?* (Qu'est-ce que c'est?)
Where is___?	*oo AY___?* (Où est___?)
Where is there___?	*oo ee-ah-t⌣EEL___* (Où y-a-t-il___?)

English	Pronunciation and French Spelling

K

kilometer	*kee-lo-METR* (kilomètre)
knife	*koo-TO* (couteau)

L

lamb	*moo-TAWNG* (mouton)
lamb chops	*kawt-LET duh moo-TAWNG* (côtelettes de mouton)
laundry	*blahn-sheess-REE* (blanchisserie)
laxative	*lak-sa-TEEF* (laxatif)
leave	
When does the train leave?	*ah KEL UR par luh TRANG?* (A quelle heure part le train?)
left	
to the left	*ah GOHSH* (à gauche)
like	
I would like	*juh voo-DRAY* (Je voudrais)
lost	*payr-DEW* (perdu)
luck	*SHAHNSS* (chance)
Good luck	*bawn SHAHNSS* (Bonne chance)

English	Pronunciation and French Spelling

M

madam	ma-DAHM (madame)
main street	grahng REW (grand'rue)
map	kraw-KEE (croquis)
Draw me a map	fet MWA ung kraw-KEE (Faites-moi un croquis)
market	mar-SHAY (marché)
matches	ah-lew-MET (allumettes)
mattress	mat-LA (matelas)
me	MWA (moi)
meat	V‿YAHND (viande)
mechanic	may-ka-neess-YANG (mécanicien)
milk	LAY (lait)
miss	mad-mwa-ZEL (mademoiselle)
moment	maw-MAHNG (moment)
Monday	LUN-DEE (lundi)
mosquito net	moo-stee-KAYR (moustiquaire)
movie	see-nay-MA (cinéma)
When does the movie start?	ah KEL UR kaw-MAHNSS luh see-nay-MA (A quelle heure commence le cinéma?)

English	Pronunciation and French Spelling

N

name

   My name is___   *juh ma-PEL.___*   (Je m'appelle___)

   What's your name?   *kaw-MAHNG voo-z_ah-puh-lay VOO?*
               (Comment vous appelez-vous?)

near   *pray* (près)

   the nearest town   *luh vee-LAJ luh plew PRAWSH*
             (le village le plus proche)

I need___   *eel muh FO___*   (Il me faut___)

needle   *ay-GWEE-yuh* (aiguille)

nine   *NUF* (neuf)

nineteen   *deez-NUF* (dix-neuf)

ninety   *kat-ruh-van-DEESS* (quatre-vingt-dix)

no   *NAWNG* (non)

north   *NAWR* (nord)

   Which way is north?   *duh kel ko-TAY ay luh NAWR?*
             (De quel côté est le nord?)

not   *ne . . . pa* (ne . . . pas)

   I do not understand   *juh nuh kawn-prahng PA* (Je ne
                comprends pas)

English	Pronunciation and French Spelling

O

of	*duh* (de)
of the	*dew* (du)
or	*duh la* (de la)
one	*UNG* (un)
o'clock	
one o'clock	*eel ay-t⌣EWN UR* (il est une heure)
two o'clock	*eel ay DUH-Z⌣UR* (il est deux heures)
oranges	*aw-RAHNJ* (oranges)

P

past	
half past six	*see-z⌣UR ay duh-MEE* (six heures et demi)
pears	*PWAR* (poires)
peas	*puh-tee PWA* (petits pois)
pen	*PLEWM* (plume)
pencil	*kray-YAWNG* (crayon)
pepper	*PWAVR* (poivre)
pillow	*aw-ray-YAY* (oreiller)
pins	*ay-PANGL* (épingles)
safety pins	*ay-PANGL duh sewr-TAY* (épingles de sûreté)

English	Pronunciation and French Spelling
pipe	*PEEP* (pipe)
plate	*ah-SYET* (assiette)
please	*seel voo PLAY* (S'il vous plaît)
policeman	*ah-JAHNG duh paw-LEESS* (agent de police)
police station	*pawst duh paw-LEESS* (poste de police)
pork	*PAWR* (porc)
pork chops	*kawt-LET duh PAWR* (côtelettes de porc)
porter	*pawr-TUR* (porteur)
post office	*bew-RO duh PAWST* (bureau de poste)
potatoes	*PAWM duh TAYR* (pommes de terre)

Q

quarter	
quarter of eight	*wee-t͜ UR mwang luh KAR* (huit heures moins le quart)
quarter past five	*sank UR ay KAR* (cinq heures et quart)
quickly	*VEET* (vite)
Come quickly!	*vuh-nay VEET!* (Venez vite!)
Go quickly!	*ah-lay VEET!* (Allez vite!)

49

English	Pronunciation and French Spelling

R

railroad	*shuh-MANG duh FAYR* (chemin de fer)
railroad station	*GAR* (gare)
Where is the railroad station?	*oo AY la GAR?* (Où est la gare?)
raincoat	*am-payr-may-ABL* (imperméable)
razor	*ra-ZWAR* (rasoir)
razor blades	*LAM duh ra-ZWAR* (lames de rasoir)
Repeat!	*ray-pay-TAY!* (Répétez!)
rest	
I want to rest	*juh VUH muh ruh-po-ZAY* (Je veux me reposer)
restaurant	*ress-to-RAHNG* (restaurant)
Where is the restaurant?	*oo AY luh ress-to-RAHNG?* (Où est le restaurant?)
rewarded	*ray-kawm-pahn-SAY* (récompensé)
You will be rewarded	*voo suh-RAY ray-kawn-pahn-SAY* (Vous serez récompensé)

English	Pronunciation and French Spelling
rice	*REE* (riz)
right	
to the right	*ah DRWAT* (à droite)
right away	*toot SWEET* (tout de suite)
river	*reev-YAYR* (rivière)
road	*root* (route)
room	*SHAHMBR* (chambre)

S

safety pins	*ay-PANGL duh sewr-TAY* (épingles de sûreté)
sailors	mah-RANG (marins)
Where are the American sailors?	oo SAWNG lay mah-RANG-Z⌣ah-may-ree-KANG? (Où sont les marins américains?)
salad	*sa-LAD* (salade)
salt	*SEL* (sel)
Saturday	*SAM-DEE* (samedi)
say	
How do you say___?	*kaw-MAHNG deet voo___?* (Comment dites-vous___?)

Versailles, the Orangery

Aigueze, Gard

English	Pronunciation and French Spelling
servant	*daw-mess-TEEK* (domestique)
seven	*SET* (sept)
seventeen	*deess-SET* (dix-sept)
seventy	*swa-sahnt-DEESS* (soixante-dix)
shave	
I want to be shaved	*juh VUII muh fayr rah-ZAY* (Je veux me faire raser)
shaving brush	*blay-RO* (blaireau)
shaving soap	*sa-VAWNG ah BARB* (savon à barbe)
she	*el* (elle)
sheets	*DRA* (draps)
shirt	*shuh-MEEZ* (chemise)
shoes	*sool-YAY* (souliers)
shoe laces	*la-SAY* (lacets)
shoe polish	*see-RAJ* (cirage)
shoemaker	*kawr-dawn-YAY* (cordonnier)
show	
Show me	*mawn-tray-MWA* (Montrez-moi)
sick	*ma-LAD* (malade)
sir	*muss-YUH* (monsieur)

English	Pronunciation and French Spelling
six	*SEESS* (six)
sixteen	*SEZ* (seize)
sixty	*swa-SAHNT* (soixante)
ship	*na-VEER*
Where is the ship?	*oo AY luh na-VEER* (Où est le navire?)
(to) sleep	*dawr-MEER* (dormir)
slowly	*lahnt-MAHNG* (lentement)
soap	*sa-VAWNG* (savon)
shaving soap	*sa-VAWNG ah BARB* · (savon à barbe)
sou	*SOO* (sou)
soup	*SOOP* (soupe)
Speak!	*par-LAY!* · (Parlez!)
Speak slowly	*par-lay lahnt-MAHNG* (Parlez lentement)
spoon	*kwee-YAYR* (cuillère)
spring (for water)	*SOORSS* (source)
starts	*kaw-MAHNSS* (commence)
When does the movie start?	*ah KEL UR kaw-MAHNSS luh see-nay-MA?* (A quelle heure commence le cinéma?)
station	
police station	*PAWST duh paw-LEESS* (poste de police)

English	Pronunciation and French Spelling
railroad station	*GAR* (gare)
Where is the railroad station?	*oo AY la GAR* (Où est la gare?)
steak	
beefsteak	*bif-TEK* (bifteck)
Stop!	*ALT!* (Halte!)
store	*ma-ga-ZANG* (magasin)
clothing store	*ma-ga-ZANG duh kawn-feks-YAWNG* (magasin de confection)
straight ahead	*too DRWA* (tout droit)
street	*rew* (rue)
main street	*grahng REW* (grand'rue)
string beans	*ah-ree-ko VAYR* (haricots verts)
sugar	*sewkr* (sucre)
Sunday	*dee-MAHNSH* (dimanche)

T

tailor	*ta-YUR* (tailleur)
take	
I want to take a bath	*juh VUH prahndr ung BANG* (Je veux prendre un bain)

English	Pronunciation and French Spelling
Take me to a doctor	*kawn-dwee-zay-MWA shay-z⁓ung dawk-TUR* (Conduisez-moi chez un docteur)
Take me to the hospital	*kawn-dwee-zay-MWA ah lo-pee-TAL* (Conduisez-moi à l'hôspital)
Take me there	*muh-nay-z⁓ee MWA* (Menez-y-moi)
tea	*TAY* (thé)
telegraph office	*bew-ro dew tay-lay-GRAF* (bureau du télégraphe)
telephone	*tay-lay-FAWN* (téléphone)
ten	*DEESS* (dix)
Thank you	*mayr-SEE* (merci)
that	
What's that?	*KESS kuh say kuh SA?* (Qu'est-ce que c'est que çà?)
the *or* *or*	*luh* (le) *lah* (la) *lay* (les)
there	
Take me there	*muh-nay-z⁓ee MWA* (Menez-y-moi)

English	Pronunciation and French Spelling
they	*eel* (ils)
They are	*eel SAWNG* (Ils sont)
thirsty	
I am thirsty	*jay SWAF* (J'ai soif)
thirteen	*TREZ* (treize)
thirty	*TRAHNT* (trente)
this	*suh-SEE* (ceci)
What's this?	*KESS kuh suh-SEE?* (Qu'est-ce que ceci?)
thousand	*MEEL* (mil)
thread	*FEEL* (fil)
three	*TRWA* (trois)
Thursday	*JUH-DEE* (jeudi)
time	
at what time	*ah kel UR* (à quelle heure)
What time is it?	*kel UR ay-t_EEL?* (Quelle heure est-il?)
tired	*fa-tee-GAY* (fatigué)
to	
to the right	*ah DRWAT* (à droite)
to the left	*ah GOHSH* (à gauche)

English	Pronunciation and French Spelling
to a doctor	*o dawk-TUR* (au docteur)
to the hospital	*ah lo-pee-TAL* (à l'hôpital)
tobacco	*ta-BA* (tabac)
today	*o-joord-WEE* (aujourd'hui)
toilet	*la-va-BO* (lavabo)
Where is the toilet?	*oo AY luh la-va-BO?* (Où est le lavabo?)
tomorrow	*duh-MANG* (demain)
too expensive	*tro SHAYR* (trop cher)
toothbrush	*BRAWSS ah DAHNG* (brosse à dents)
tooth paste	*PAHT dahn-tee-FREESS* (pâte dentifrice)
towel	*sayrv-YET* (serviette)
town	*vee-LAJ* (village)
the nearest town	*luh vee-LAJ luh plew PRAWSH* (le village le plus proche)
train	*TRANG* (train)
When does the train leave?	*ah KEL UR par luh TRANG?* (A quelle heure part le train?)
Tuesday	*MAR-DEE* (mardi)
twelve	*DOOZ* (douze)

English	Pronunciation and French Spelling
twenty	*VANG* (vingt)
twenty-one	*van-t͜ay UNG* (vingt-et-un)
twenty-two	*vant-DUH* (vingt-deux)
two	*DUH* (deux)

U

understand	
Do you understand?	*KAWM-pruh-nay VOO?* (Comprenez-vous?)
I understand	*juh kawm-PRAHNG* (Je comprends)
I don't understand	*juh nuh KAWM-prahng PA* (Je ne comprends pas)
underwear	*soo-vet-MAHNG* (sous-vêtements)

V

veal	*vo* (veau)
vegetables	*lay-GEWM* (légumes)

W

Wait!	*ah-tahn-DAY!* (Attendez!)
Wait a moment	*ah-tahn-DAY-Z͜ung mo-MAHNG* (Attendez un moment)

English	Pronunciation and French Spelling
want	
I want__ *or*	
I want to__	*juh VUH__* (Je veux__)
We want__	*noo voo-LAWNG__* (Nous voulons__)
wash up	
I want to wash up	*juh VUH muh la-VAY* (Je veux me laver
Watch out!	*pruh-nay GARD!* (Prenez garde!)
water	*O* (eau)
boiled water	*O boo-YEE* (eau bouillie)
drinking water	*O paw-TABL* (eau potable)
hot water	*o SHOHD* (eau chaude)
we	*NOO* (nous)
We are__	*noo SAWM__* (Nous sommes__)
We have__	*noo-z_ah-VAWNG__* (Nous avons__)
We don't have__	*noo na-vawng PA__* (Nous n'avons pas__)
We want__	*noo voo-LAWNG__* (Nous voulons__)
Wednesday	*MAYR-kruh-DEE* (mercredi)
well (for water)	*pwee* (puits)

59

English	Pronunciation and French Spelling
welcome	
You're welcome	*eel nee ah pa duh KWA* (Il n'y a pas de quoi)
what	
What is it?	*kess kuh SAY?* (Qu'est-ce que c'est?)
What's this?	*KESS kuh suh-SEE?* (Qu'est-ce que ceci?)
What's that?	*KESS kuh say kuh SAH?* (Qu'est-ce que c'est que çà?)
What is your name?	*kaw-MAHNG voo-z_ah-puh-lay VOO?* (Comment vous appelez-vous?)
What time is it?	*kel UR ay-t_EEL?* (Quelle heure est-il?)
when	*KAHNG* (quand)
When does the movie start?	*ah KEL UR kaw-MAHNSS luh see-nay-MA?* (A quelle heure commence le cinéma?)
When does the train leave?	*ah KEL UR par luh TRANG?* (A quelle heure part le train?)
where	*oo* (où)
Where is___?	*oo AY___?* (Où est___?)
Where are___?	*oo SAWNG___?* (Où sont___?)

English	Pronunciation and French Spelling
Where is there___?	*oo ee-ah-t_EEL___?* (Où y a-t-il___?)
which	
Which is the road to___?	*kel ay luh shuh-MANG poor___?* (Quel est le chemin pour___?)
Which way is north?	*duh kel ko-TAY ay luh NAWR?* (De quel côté est le nord?)
wine	*vang* (vin)
a bottle of wine	*ewn boo-TAY_ee duh VANG* (une bouteille de vin)
workman	*oov-R_YAY* (ouvrier)
wounded	*blay-SAY* (blessé)

Y

yes	*wee* (oui)
yesterday	*ee-YAYR* (hier)
you	*voo* (vous)
You will be rewarded	*voo suh-RAY ray-kawm-pahn-SAY* (Vous serez récompensé)
Have you?	*ah-vay VOO?* (Avez-vous?)
Are you?	*et VOO?* (Etes-vous?)

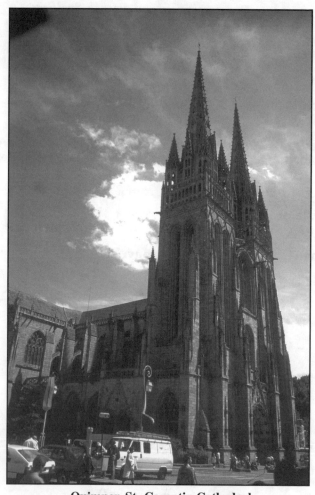

Quimper, St.-Corentin Cathedral